Lessons

in

Deliverance

Loren VanGalder

Spiritual Father Publications

Table of Contents

Introduction

A significant part of Jesus' ministry involved deliverance from unclean spirits – primarily with God's chosen people who were living in a religious society. Jesus sent his disciples out with authority to free people from demons – and they did. Deliverance continued to be an important part of the early church's ministry.

Today we often think of deliverance as the theatrics of exorcisms in the movies. Although the Catholic church officially believes in (and practices) exorcism, and Pentecostal churches are often known for dramatic deliverances, it is not a regular part of most churches' ministry. Why? Has demonic activity diminished since Jesus' day? I would argue the opposite: In our secular world I believe there is far more demonic activity than at any other time in history. I ministered for 21 years as a chaplain in federal prisons, which are full of people oppressed by the devil. I constantly see evidence of demonization – often in church!

How about you? Do you believe in deliverance? Most Christians are uncomfortable with it, and unequipped to minister to the demonized. What's worse, most pastors aren't much better off. Others go overboard and see demons everywhere. Balanced teaching is hard to find, with the secular media and personal experience overshadowing Scripture. What better teacher than Jesus?

Deliverance is not an easy ministry. It would be tempting to simply ignore it, but to do so leaves multitudes of people downtrodden by evil satanic forces. Jesus expected deliverance to be part of his disciples' ministry, and was disappointed when they couldn't deliver; he attributed their failure to a lack of faith, prayer, and fasting. Any Spirit-filled believer with vibrant faith has authority over evil spirits. Unlike healing, there is no specific spiritual gift, although the gift of discernment of spirits is helpful.

Not a great deal is written about deliverance in the New Testament, and there are no clear teaching passages, but we will look at every deliverance recorded in the Gospels and Acts. I pray this would give you the courage to step forth in your God-given authority and be an instrument God can use to free people, and lead them into the fullness of the Spirit-empowered life.

1 Know when to get into your boat – and when to get out

Mark 5:1-20

¹So they arrived at the other side of the lake, in the region of the Gerasenes. ² When Jesus climbed out of the boat, a man possessed by an evil spirit came out from a cemetery to meet him.

Do you want the Lord to use you? Sometimes we stay at home, praying "What do you want me to do? Show me your will." It certainly can be appropriate to wait for God to clearly guide you, but sometimes you may just need to get into the boat and go with Jesus. When you go with him, you never know what is going to happen. Sometimes you have to go to the other side, to a place nobody wants to go. The Jews never went to the Decapolis, the region of the Gerasenes, ten gentile cities on the east side of the Jordan. For the disciples, this was one more un-asked-for adventure, like the time they went with Jesus through Samaria. We know Jesus wasn't alone: It says *they* arrived, but that's the last we hear of the disciples. From then on it was just Jesus dealing with the people; the disciples probably stayed in the boat. When Jesus climbs out, don't stay in the boat unless he tells you to, even if it's somewhere you really don't want to be.

Jesus may tell you where you are going, and why, but many times he doesn't. Jesus often knew, but in this case I suspect he didn't. He hadn't arranged any meetings. Probably nobody knew him; his reputation had not reached that far east. He went in obedience to his father, and we will see that the whole trip was for just one man, like Philip was sent through the desert to speak with the Ethiopian eunuch (Acts 8:26-40). Are you willing to do that? If his Spirit is leading you, trust God to send you people he has prepared, even if they are not who you expected to minister to.

3 This man lived among the burial caves and could no longer be restrained, even with a chain. 4 Whenever he was put into chains and shackles—as he often was—he snapped the chains from his wrists and smashed the shackles. No one was strong enough to subdue him.5 Day and night he wandered among the burial caves and in the hills, howling and cutting himself with sharp stones.

Can you recognize the demonized person?

The devil came to steal, kill, and destroy. Don't be deceived; he is real, and the Bible clearly speaks about evil spirits and demonized people. Sometimes it is very obvious, as in this case. They may be self-destructive and uncontrollable, but this is extreme: He had thousands of demons. It is very possible that there are demonized people around you. Do you know what to do if one approaches you, as this man approached Jesus? In the Bible, neither Jesus nor the apostles went looking for demons. In fact, they usually tried to avoid them, but they clearly had the power to cast them out. God wants to equip his servants to minister to people tormented by demons.

⁶ *When Jesus was still some distance away, the man saw him, ran to meet him, and bowed low before him.* ⁷ *With a shriek, he screamed, "Why are you interfering with me, Jesus, Son of the Most High God? In the name of God, I beg you, don't torture me!"* ⁸ *For Jesus had already said to the spirit, "Come out of the man, you evil spirit."*

⁹ *Then Jesus demanded, "What is your name?"*

And he replied, "My name is Legion, because there are many of us inside this man." ¹⁰ *Then the evil spirits begged him again and again not to send them to some distant place.*

¹¹ *There happened to be a large herd of pigs feeding on the hillside nearby.* ¹² *"Send us into those pigs," the spirits begged. "Let us enter them."*

¹³ *So Jesus gave them permission. The evil spirits came out of the man and entered the pigs, and the entire herd of about 2,000 pigs plunged down the steep hillside into the lake and drowned in the water.*

Jesus' surprising interaction with demons

Does it surprise you that the demons went running *towards* Jesus? Wouldn't you expect them to run *away* from him? But they know him! They had been with him in heaven! And they pray to him! They knew he had authority over them. They had been fine dwelling in this poor man, and didn't want to go to some desolate place. And Jesus honors their request! Of course, as a good Jew, Jesus wasn't too fond of pigs. But it is interesting that he gave them what they wanted.

Jesus didn't know the demon's name, or how many there were. The practice of talking with demons and asking their names during deliverance is partly based on Jesus' example here, but be careful: They are liars and deceivers. Use great discernment when talking with a demonized person.

Did you notice the spirit didn't come out when Jesus first commanded him to leave? Jesus never did cast them out – but they needed his permission to enter the pigs. Once he gave that, they left the man on their own. It was all a question of authority.

What happened to the demons once the pigs drowned? We don't know, but I suspect the demons were not expecting that to happen. It is possible that the pigs' death released them to go back to the heavenly realms to await their next assignment, just as they leave a person who dies.

14 The herdsmen fled to the nearby town and the surrounding countryside, spreading the news as they ran. People rushed out to see what had happened.15 A crowd soon gathered around Jesus, and they saw the man who had been possessed by the legion of demons. He was sitting there fully clothed and perfectly sane, and they were all afraid.16 Then those who had seen what happened told the others about the demon-possessed man and the pigs.17 And the crowd began pleading with Jesus to go away and leave them alone.

Know when to leave

Leave them alone? Some translations say *leave them in peace.* Were they really in peace? Were they really better off before Jesus came? Were they more concerned about their pigs than about this man? Why weren't they worshipping Jesus and seeking more of his power? Yet that is how many people respond when they come face to face with God's power. Sometimes their sin is exposed, or they recognize something supernatural, and are afraid.

It can be hard to know when to persevere and keep preaching to people who have rejected the Gospel. You must be guided by the Spirit and discern what is happening. This was clearly a closed door. God loved this poor man and had Jesus come all that way just to set him free, but it was the only ministry he had in that place. Nothing would have happened had he invested more time or money.

¹⁸ As Jesus was getting into the boat, the man who had been demon possessed begged to go with him.¹⁹ But Jesus said, "No, go home to your family, and tell them everything the Lord has done for you and how merciful he has been." ²⁰ So the man started off to visit the Ten Towns of that region and began to proclaim the great things Jesus had done for him; and everyone was amazed at what he told them.

Let Jesus use you

Jesus did what the people asked him to do: He got into his boat. Now it was the man who came to him with a request: He begged to go with Jesus. That's great! Jesus often commanded people to follow him. But not this time. Jesus wouldn't let him in the boat. God had a mission for him.

That crazy man was one of the first evangelists. He went back to his family and proclaimed what Jesus had done throughout the entire Decapolis. He had none of the disciples' training. He had just spent years in a horrendous situation. But God restored him and equipped him to preach, and people who probably would never have listened to Jesus received him. Obviously there are times when God sends us to another country and culture, but often it is more effective to send someone God has redeemed and prepared back to their own people. They already know the language and culture.

If God could powerfully use this man to share the Gospel, what is your excuse? A simple testimony of what Jesus has done in your life can be enough to point someone to the Lord.

Get into the boat!

We have to know when to get in the boat, and when to get out. If you want the Lord to use you, many times you have to get up, get into the boat, and head out on the waters, even when you have no idea where you're going. If you arrive somewhere really different, with no idea of what to do, don't be afraid. Don't stay in the boat. God can't you use in the boat. Get out and trust the Lord to show you his purpose. Prepare yourself for whatever ministry you may encounter. And when it's time to get back in the boat and leave that place, don't hang around. Someone may want to go with you who needs to stay there to minister. People may beg you to stay, or they may slam the door in your face. Going with Jesus is an adventure! If you are bored, maybe it's time to shut the TV and computer off, get off the couch, and get into the boat!

2 Why can't I drive out a demon?

Mark 9: 2, 14-29

After six days Jesus took Peter, James and John with him and led them up a high mountain, where they were all alone. There he was transfigured before them. (Mark 9:2, NIV)

This was a special day for Jesus; one of the most glorious moments of his earthly life. It is always good to climb a mountain with friends. This was a *high* mountain, and Jesus was with his three closest friends, who would behold his glory while he conversed with Moses and Elijah!

But it wasn't such a great day for the other disciples, the ones Jesus left at the base of the mountain. With the Gadarene (Mark 5) we never saw the disciples leave the boat. Hopefully they learned from that experience, because this time it's Jesus who is out of sight, up on the mountain. They are left alone to deal with a demonized boy, and when Jesus came down from the mountain, things are not going well:

¹⁴When they came to the other disciples, they saw a large crowd around them and the teachers of the law arguing with them. ¹⁵ As soon as all the people saw Jesus, they were overwhelmed with wonder and ran to greet him.

Jesus rescues his disciples

It's rough coming down from a mountain top experience to find those you have entrusted with the work floundering. Moses had a similar experience when he descended Mount Sinai. Just as Moses' face reflected God's glorious presence, I suspect traces of glory remained on Jesus' face, which caused the people to be overwhelmed with wonder. The Amplified Bible takes the liberty of inserting that in the text: *[His face and person yet glistening]*. The other disciples were happy to see him. We don't know why the teachers of the law were arguing with them, but the issue was a demonized boy the disciples couldn't help. Perhaps the teachers took the opportunity to attack Jesus' credibility in general, and the disciples rushed to his defense.

[16] "What are you arguing with them about?" Jesus asked.

[17] A man in the crowd answered, "Teacher, I brought you my son, who is possessed by a spirit that has robbed him of speech. [18] Whenever it seizes him, it throws him to the ground. He foams at the mouth, gnashes his teeth and becomes rigid. I asked your disciples to drive out the spirit, but they could not."

Have you seen that? Or experienced it? People have to settle for help from a young pastor (perhaps an assistant, or youth pastor) who is left in charge, while the person they really want to see (the senior pastor, or well-known evangelist) is unavailable. Except that person doesn't seem to have the same anointing, and can't help them. It is a humiliating experience for the one who fails, and perhaps even worse for these disciples, since Peter, James, and John witnessed it. This father came with a simple request to drive out the evil spirit, and the disciples couldn't deliver.

It's not they were inexperienced in deliverance, or lacked authority over evil spirits. Jesus had already given them authority to cast out demons, and they had considerable success doing so on their first missionary journey:

And he called his twelve disciples together and began sending them out two by two, giving them authority to cast out evil spirits. So the disciples went out, telling everyone they met to repent of their sins and turn to God. And they cast out many demons and healed many sick people, anointing them with olive oil. (Mark 6:7, 12-13, NLT)

But this time it was different. What is some of the evidence of demonization in this young boy?

Symptoms of demonization

- A person tormented by a spirit may be fine much of the time, but it may manifest without warning.
- There can also be an ongoing affliction, such as being unable to speak, that would often be explained as psychological or physical.
- When a demon manifests, the person may:
  - Be thrown to the ground; the Amplified adds *convulses him.*
  - Foam at the mouth.
  - Gnash his teeth.
  - Become rigid.

Is it spiritual or medical?

These symptoms could easily be mistaken for a seizure, which raises a key dilemma in deliverance: When is it a demon, and when is it an illness? Do you administer medicine, or cast out the demon? Modern science often ridicules Christians who attribute these symptoms to the devil. Undoubtedly, many can be explained medically; it is unwise to ascribe every case to a demon and rule out medical knowledge. Yet it seems the pendulum has swung too far to the other side: Even Christians rarely look for the spiritual reason behind the problem. What about the alarming rise in autism, auto-immune diseases, and other afflictions that baffle the medical establishment? Are millions of people suffering needlessly because Christians lack the authority and boldness to confront the demons behind them? We obviously want to avoid extremes, but Jesus had no problem attributing these symptoms to demons, and his approach provided immediate relief.

[19] *"You unbelieving generation," Jesus replied, "how long shall I stay with you? How long shall I put up with you? Bring the boy to me."*

An unbelieving, perverse generation

After Jesus' taste of heaven on the mountain, he finds their lack of faith even more disturbing. This is one of the few times Jesus shows impatience and a struggle with being on earth. He probably would have preferred staying on the mountain, or going straight home to heaven. The parallel passage in Matthew (17:17) adds *perverse* to his description of the disciples. He is not sympathetic to their plight. He expected them to help the boy. How would Jesus describe our generation? It seems there is at least as much unbelief among us.

[20] *So they brought him. When the spirit saw Jesus, it immediately threw the boy into a convulsion. He fell to the ground and rolled around, foaming at the mouth.*

Get informed

In Jesus' presence the spirit immediately manifested. Why were there no manifestations around the disciples? Is it possible we see few such manifestations because spirits don't sense God's presence in us? Instead of getting better, initially the boy got worse. Some parents would grab him and run for the nearest hospital. Some pastors would panic and immediately try to get control of the situation. But Jesus calmly asks for further clarification, apparently while the boy rolled around on the ground in convulsions.

[21] *Jesus asked the boy's father, "How long has he been like this?"*

"From childhood," he answered. [22] *"It has often thrown him into fire or water to kill him. But if you can do anything, take pity on us and help us."*

Why did Jesus want to know this? Perhaps he could tell the demon was deeply attached and had been there a long time? This does seem like an especially strong case. Or perhaps he wanted to connect with the father in some way, to give him a chance to express his pain over his son's condition.

Demons often enter because of some sin or experience that opens the door and leaves the person vulnerable. But if this boy had been demonized since childhood, it may have been passed down from his parents.

Have you known accident-prone people? They seem to have a death wish, and constantly end up in dramatic situations. Pay attention to that. Demons are bent on destruction, and often are successful at killing the person they possess. Don't take it lightly, and don't belittle the person as being attention-seeking or overly dramatic.

It took faith for the father to bring the boy to Jesus, but now he betrays doubt. Possibly because the other disciples have already failed, he's not sure if Jesus can help either. Maybe you have been let down by a pastor you thought could help you, and now your faith in God (or, especially, in his servants), is shaken. Don't let others' lack of faith weaken yours!

23 "'If you can'?" said Jesus. "Everything is possible for one who believes."

Everything is possible

Jesus seems displeased at this expression of doubt. The faith he rewards and seeks is a broad faith that realizes anything is possible if we just believe. Do you come to Jesus with that wimpy "if you can" attitude? Or with bold faith? This is one of a number of statements Jesus makes that gives practically unlimited resources to the one who truly believes.

24 Immediately the boy's father exclaimed, "I do believe; help me overcome my unbelief!"

At least the father is honest. He probably sensed Jesus' irritation at his doubt and was afraid of missing any chance to help his son. If you struggle with doubt and unbelief, you are not alone. Go to God and ask his help in overcoming your unbelief. Learn to recognize your doubts and challenge them. Be honest – God already knows about them, and can still work despite our doubts. The father's doubt didn't keep Jesus from doing this miracle.

25 When Jesus saw that a crowd was running to the scene, he rebuked the impure spirit. "You deaf and mute spirit," he said, "I command you, come out of him and never enter him again."

Challenging the evil spirit

Perhaps Jesus would have continued talking with the father, but the boy was attracting too much attention, and he realized it was time to stop it. Don't let deliverances become a show! Be sensitive to the poor person rolling around on the floor! Don't put it on TV or the internet!

- This wasn't mentioned before, but the same spirit that robbed his speech, robbed his hearing. Some cultures shun deaf people because they believe they are all demon possessed. Don't shun them! Deliver them!
- Jesus rebuked the spirit and then commanded it to come out. There was no pleading or long debate. Jesus had authority to command it to leave – and you have been given that same authority.
- There is a second part to the command that is often overlooked. Had Jesus not commanded the demon to never return, there is a good chance it would. When a spirit has dwelt in someone that long, it will be inclined to return. I have seen that happen. Follow-up is critical after deliverance. If we are not careful, the person can end up worse than before: *"When an impure spirit comes out of a person, it goes through arid places seeking rest and does not find it. Then it says, 'I will return to the house I left.' When it arrives, it finds the house swept clean and put in order. Then it goes and takes*

seven other spirits more wicked than itself, and they go in and live there. And the final condition of that person is worse than the first." (Jesus, Luke 11:24-26) Then people question whether the deliverance was real and may give up on a spiritual approach altogether.

[26] The spirit shrieked, convulsed him violently and came out. The boy looked so much like a corpse that many said, "He's dead." [27] But Jesus took him by the hand and lifted him to his feet, and he stood up.

The results of deliverance

Expect dramatic physical manifestations, but don't leave him lying there! Reach out, take his hand, and lift him up! Keep ministering to him until he has recovered. Deliverance can be traumatic!

It doesn't say what happened afterward, but we can surmise:

- The doubting father had his faith strengthened.
- The argumentative teachers of the law were silenced.
- The crowd that was already in awe of Jesus was probably more amazed.

But Jesus apparently didn't take advantage of the situation to ask if anyone else needed deliverance, or wanted to follow him. He seems to have slipped away with his disciples, perhaps drained by the encounter, and still thinking about his glorious transfiguration.

[28] After Jesus had gone indoors, his disciples asked him privately, "Why couldn't we drive it out?"

[29] He replied, *"This kind can come out only by prayer and fasting."*

Why can't we drive out a demon?

The three who had been with Jesus on the mountain were instructed not to tell anyone about the transfiguration, but the other disciples didn't even inquire; they were too wrapped up with their wounded pride. What went wrong? How could Jesus do it so effortlessly? The debriefing takes place away from the crowd, inside a house.

Jesus suggests there are various levels of difficulty in deliverance. This was a hard case. You need discernment to know how to approach each situation. Does this mean you spend time in prayer and fasting before attempting a deliverance? Possibly - but Jesus didn't. What were the disciples supposed to say when the father brought his son to them? Come back tomorrow? We need to pray and fast first? Ideally, we would be "prayed up" and strengthened through regular fasting, so we are ready to confront whatever comes our way. If you are not, it may be better to arrange a later meeting so you can be adequately prepared, and avoid the disciples' humiliation. It never hurts to call in reinforcements. I have found it is usually better to have several people ministering deliverance, especially if you are united in the Spirit. Jesus allowed no room for failure just because this was a severe case. We should expect deliverance for every demonized person.

The parallel passage in Matthew (17:20) includes another part of Jesus' explanation that Mark omits:

He replied, "Because you have so little faith. Truly I tell you, if you have faith as small as a mustard seed, you can say to this mountain, 'Move from here to there,' and it will move. Nothing will be impossible for you."

This reflects Jesus' initial dismay at the *"unbelieving and perverse generation."* He takes advantage of the situation to give a general teaching on the unlimited possibilities for the one who has faith, and places our failures in deliverance squarely on our lack of faith. Along with a lack of prayer and fasting, that explains why we find it difficult to discern the presence of evil spirits, let alone cast them out.

Are you ready for God to use you?

- How is your faith? Don't wait until you are put to the test, and embarrassed because you can't deliver someone. Do you have faith that God has given you authority over evil spirits? Do you have the faith to step out and command them to leave?
- What has been your experience in deliverance? Has unbalanced teaching or failure caused you to avoid it? Do you think God might want you to take it more seriously?
- Is someone's deliverance important enough to you to spend the necessary time in prayer and fasting to help them?
- Are there people – perhaps even in your own family – who are suffering because they are afflicted by evil spirits? Have you tried all kinds of doctors and therapy – without success? Are you ready to consider the possibility of demonization? If it is someone close to you – or yourself – can you see where the door might have been opened to a demon?

- God may give you a test case this week. Are you ready?

One more thing I want to mention: There is a lot of argument in the church about whether a Christian can be "demon possessed." The Greek New Testament doesn't speak of possession; it talks about a person being "demonized" – afflicted by a demon. Whether it is from inside or outside, the effect can be the same. Don't get distracted from the real issue by getting caught up in that argument.

3   The Authority of a Word

The only records of deliverances found in all three synoptic gospels are Jesus' deliverance of Legion, the Gadarene (Matthew 8:28-32, Mark 5:1-20, and Luke 8:26-39), and the boy the disciples couldn't help (Matthew 17:14-21, Mark 9:14-29, and Luke 9:37-43). There are none recorded in John. In this chapter we will look at several shorter Gospel passages, and the one deliverance recorded in Acts.

The power of a word

When evening came, many who were demon-possessed were brought to him, and he drove out the spirits with a word and healed all the sick. (Matthew 8:16)

Mark's account (1:32-34) of the same evening adds more detail:

That evening after sunset the people brought to Jesus all the sick and demon-possessed. The whole town gathered at the door, and Jesus healed many who had various diseases. He also drove out many demons, but he would not let the demons speak because they knew who he was.

No wonder they *all* came, and brought *all* the sick and demon-possessed. Who would pass up that opportunity? Mark says he healed *many;* Matthew says he healed *all*. It is safe to assume that no one who came demonized or sick left without a miracle.

The needy were *brought* by friends or relatives. Perhaps they were unable or unwilling to seek help on their own. Like the friends who brought the paralytic and lowered him through the roof, others' faith was at least as important as the sick person's. Do you know anyone you should bring to Jesus for healing or deliverance? Don't leave them at home sick or bound up by demons! Jesus is waiting to heal them!

Demons know Jesus, and they are not afraid to talk about him, but Jesus doesn't need that kind of testimony. He has authority to drive them out, and he has authority to silence them. There was no protracted struggle, anointing with oil, or conversations with the demons; he simply drove them out with a word.

Do you find that striking? Someone who has been devastated by demonic oppression or illness for years can have their life turned around by a *word*. It all depends on who is speaking that word, and what authority is backing them up. If you are submitted to God and believe he has given you authority, speak his word. It is sufficient to deliver or heal.

Expect opposition

While they were going out, a man who was demon-possessed and could not talk was brought to Jesus. And when the demon was driven out, the man who had been mute spoke. The crowd was amazed and said, "Nothing like this has ever been seen in Israel."

But the Pharisees said, "It is by the prince of demons that he drives out demons." (Matthew 9:32-34)

Once again, a demon is robbing someone of their speech. The people were familiar with demon possession, but they had no hope of help until Jesus came. Most people will be amazed at God's power, but then, as now, it is often religious people who oppose deliverance – probably because it exposes their own lack of spiritual power. As Jesus said elsewhere, it makes no sense for Satan to drive out his own demons. He may conjure up counterfeit miracles, but genuine deliverance only comes from God. Witch doctors and others who supposedly offer relief from demonization apart from Jesus do not provide real deliverance.

Authority and power

Then he went down to Capernaum, a town in Galilee, and on the Sabbath he taught the people. They were amazed at his teaching, because his words had authority.

In the synagogue there was a man possessed by a demon, an impure spirit. He cried out at the top of his voice, "Go away! What do you want with us, Jesus of Nazareth? Have you come to destroy us? I know who you are—the Holy One of God!"

"Be quiet!" Jesus said sternly. "Come out of him!" Then the demon threw the man down before them all and came out without injuring him.

All the people were amazed and said to each other, "What words these are! With authority and power he gives orders to impure spirits and they come out!" And the news about him spread throughout the surrounding area. (Luke 4:31-37)

Jesus' authority is impressive. First, the people noticed it in his teaching, then the demon recognized it, and by the end of the service everyone was marveling at Jesus' authority over the unclean spirit. Jesus wasn't conducting a deliverance service or seeking opportunities to free people from their demons, but when the situation arises, Jesus calmly – but sternly – deals with it immediately. The demon knew Jesus before Satan was tossed out of heaven along with a third of the angels. He knows Jesus is bad news for him, and expects to be destroyed. He speaks of himself in the plural, probably indicating more than one demon. That is usually the case.

Demons will try to disrupt church services. They tend to be noisy; he yelled at the top of his voice. If the person can't be dealt with quickly, they should be removed and ministered to out of sight. Again, Jesus doesn't get into a conversation with the demon, and he doesn't allow it to "testify" about who he is. Simple words of authority drive it out, but not without a struggle, as it threw the man to the floor.

It is curious that the man was even in the synagogue. Apparently the demon was comfortable there. The people weren't used to authoritative preaching or ministry. Instead of the demon compelling the man to leave, he tries to get Jesus to go! Demons may be present in our churches, and will do anything possible to remove a believer anointed with God's authority who can disrupt them.

"Be quiet! Come out of him!" Could you say those words with the same effect? Absolutely! It has nothing to do with a formula or using exactly the right words. It has everything to do with your relationship to God, your submission to him, and the resulting authority as you speak in faith.

Remote deliverance

Leaving that place, Jesus withdrew to the region of Tyre and Sidon. A Canaanite woman from that vicinity came to him, crying out, "Lord, Son of David, have mercy on me! My daughter is demon-possessed and suffering terribly."

Jesus did not answer a word. So his disciples came to him and urged him, "Send her away, for she keeps crying out after us."

He answered, "I was sent only to the lost sheep of Israel."

The woman came and knelt before him. "Lord, help me!" she said.

He replied, "It is not right to take the children's bread and toss it to the dogs."

"Yes it is, Lord," she said. "Even the dogs eat the crumbs that fall from their master's table."

Then Jesus said to her, "Woman, you have great faith! Your request is granted." And her daughter was healed at that moment. (Matthew 15:21-28, also found in Mark 7:24-30)

This is a remarkable situation:

- Jesus and his disciples are in Gentile territory. They have *"withdrawn"* there to get away from the crowds and get some rest. Mark says *He entered a house and did not want anyone to know it; yet he could not keep his presence secret.*

- A Gentile, Canaanite woman (Mark: *a Greek, born in Syrian Phoenicia*) somehow knows about Jesus and is determined to get his help. She keeps pestering him until the disciples ask Jesus to send her away. It is interesting that they don't feel they have the authority to speak to her, perhaps because they were in foreign territory.

- Jesus appears rude. First he ignores her. It is the only time he refuses to even answer someone who sincerely comes to him looking for help. Then he essentially calls her a dog. He reflects the worst prejudice of the time toward Gentiles. The disciples are no better. Instead of interceding for her, they want to send her away! Why would Jesus act like this? He was very aware of the mission given him by his Father and wanted to stay faithful to it (Mark: *"First let the children eat all they want"*). He knew the time would come when Gentiles would be included – but not yet.

- This was a remote deliverance – the girl wasn't even present.

What moved Jesus to act? The woman's great faith. Why would he say it was great? Was it some kind of feeling she worked up? Not at all. She had full confidence Jesus could help her, and wouldn't give up until he did. Despite the disciples' attempts to silence her, she persisted in crying out, and eventually came and knelt at Jesus' feet. And she contradicts Jesus! He said it's *not* right – and she said it *is* right! All she wanted was crumbs! Like mustard seed faith! That perceptive, bold, faith-filled response moved Jesus' heart (Mark: *"For such a reply, you may go; the demon has left your daughter."*). Her faith is further evidenced by believing what Jesus said, and leaving him (instead of asking him to come to the house, or seeking some further assurance): *She went home and found her child lying on the bed, and the demon gone.* (Mark 7:30)

When we are dealing in the spirit realm, there is no need to be physically present. Everything is done in the spirit. There is no reason to doubt that, no matter where they, Jesus could deliver your son, daughter, or other loved one. Do you have the faith and persistence to keep crying out to Jesus? Do you really believe he is going to do what he said he would do?

Bound for eighteen years

On a Sabbath Jesus was teaching in one of the synagogues, and a woman was there who had been crippled by a spirit for eighteen years. She was bent over and could not straighten up at all. When Jesus saw her, he called her forward and said to her, "Woman, you are set free from your infirmity." Then he put his hands on her, and immediately she straightened up and praised God.

Indignant because Jesus had healed on the Sabbath, the synagogue leader said to the people, "There are six days for work. So come and be healed on those days, not on the Sabbath."

The Lord answered him, "You hypocrites! Doesn't each of you on the Sabbath untie your ox or donkey from the stall and lead it out to give it water? Then should not this woman, a daughter of Abraham, whom Satan has kept bound for eighteen long years, be set free on the Sabbath day from what bound her?" (Luke 13:10-16)

While Jesus ignored the Canaanite woman who was seeking help, here he calls out a woman who didn't even ask for help, and shows no indication of faith for deliverance. Indeed, she had been bound by Satan for eighteen years, and hope was long gone. She was probably a regular attendee at synagogue, but apparently that didn't trouble the demon. Several things are noteworthy:

- This is the only example in the Gospels where Jesus laid hands on someone for deliverance.

- He doesn't command the demon to leave (and it would seem to be pretty deeply entrenched after eighteen years), but simply tells the woman she is set free.

- The spirit had crippled her. Do we even consider the possibility that a physically impaired person might be demonized?

- Initially it is called a spirit – then Jesus says it is Satan who bound her. They work together; demons get their authority from Satan.

- Once again, the opposition comes from a religious leader, whom Jesus calls a hypocrite!

She straightened up and praised God! I like that! Would you be willing to call someone out so they could get free from their bondages? Do you have the discernment to recognize when it is a spiritual bondage? Is it time for you to leave whatever is binding you, to straighten up, and start praising God? It's never too late! Eighteen years is a long time – but in a moment she was made whole.

The disciples' experience in deliverance

Little is said about the disciples – but the accounts indicate considerable success in deliverance (except for their failure with that poor boy!).

Calling the Twelve to him, he began to send them out two by two and gave them authority over impure spirits. They drove out many demons and anointed many sick people with oil and healed them. (Mark 6:7, 13)

When Jesus had called the Twelve together, he gave them power and authority to drive out all demons and to cure diseases. (Luke 9:1)

They were *given* all they needed for ministry: Jesus' power and authority, which was given him by his Father, and exercised through the power of the Holy Spirit. He *gives* it to us. You can't earn it, and it doesn't require any special status. It is given to Jesus' followers. Too bad so few realize what they have!

Jesus didn't specifically commission the seventy-two to cast out demons, yet they did:

The seventy-two returned with joy and said, "Lord, even the demons submit to us in your name."

He replied, "I saw Satan fall like lightning from heaven. I have given you authority to trample on snakes and scorpions and to overcome all the power of the enemy; nothing will harm you. However, do not rejoice that the spirits submit to you, but rejoice that your names are written in heaven." (Luke 10:17-20)

The disciples were learning the power of Jesus' name. Demons have to submit to that name. That can get heady for us, and Jesus has a word of caution: Satan got carried away with the power God had given him, and it led to his fall. We need to be careful of getting carried away with deliverance ministry, and keep our focus on Jesus, and his gift of salvation.

In the meantime, grab onto this promise: The enemy cannot harm you. Jesus has given us authority not only to overcome *all* the enemy's power, but to trample on evil spirits. Do you have some trampling to do? Have you been intimidated by Satan? Even hurt by him? Are you ready to rise up in the authority Jesus has given you?

Crowds gathered also from the towns around Jerusalem, bringing their sick and those tormented by impure spirits, and all of them were healed. (Acts 5:16)

Exactly like Jesus, *all* those tormented by impure spirits were healed. They may not have come on their own, but were *brought* to the disciples. When healing and deliverance are ministered, crowds will come.

Deliverance lands them in jail

Once when we were going to the place of prayer, we were met by a female slave who had a spirit by which she predicted the future. She earned a great deal of money for her owners by fortune-telling. She followed Paul and the rest of us, shouting, "These men are servants of the Most High God, who are telling you the way to be saved." She kept this up for many days. Finally Paul became so annoyed that he turned around and said to the spirit, "In the name of Jesus

Christ I command you to come out of her!" At that moment the spirit left her. (Acts 16:16-18)

Be careful of fortune-tellers – and even those who claim a "prophetic gift" to predict the future. There can be an evil spirit behind it! Just as several demonized people came to Jesus, this woman is drawn to Paul, and is disrupting his ministry. I don't know why Paul would wait so long to deal with her. Maybe he knew it could cause further trouble. Read all of Acts 16 and you will find it led them straight to jail. It is interesting to see Paul ministering out of annoyance instead of love, but as he speaks "in the name of Jesus Christ" it is just like Jesus was there. He has the same authority. And at a simple word, the spirit leaves her.

I believe there are countless people out there like the Canaanite's daughter and the crippled woman. Many of them are in church. They have no idea that their affliction is caused by a demon. As in Jesus' day, many religious people have unwittingly been used by Satan himself to ridicule and discount the deliverance ministry. As can be expected, there have been abuses, but be careful of ignoring an important part of what Jesus came to do. Keep your eyes open this week. How is your faith? Do you really believe Jesus has authority? Do you believe what he said? He needs someone to speak the word, to command the spirit to leave. Are you available for him to use?

4   The Strong Man

Matthew 12:22-37

This is Jesus' longest teaching on deliverance. As we have seen repeatedly, his focus was on the Kingdom of God. He only dealt with Satan when he had to. We would do well to keep our focus on the Lord and not give the devil more attention than absolutely necessary. We can tend to think of the spiritual war as a battle between equals, but Satan is not omniscient, omnipresent, or omnipotent — he is a fallen angel, created by God, and under God's control.

Healing or deliverance?

22Then they brought him a demon-possessed man who was blind and mute, and Jesus healed him, so that he could both talk and see. 23All the people were astonished and said, "Could this be the Son of David?"

Are deliverance and healing the same thing? They certainly are closely related. Sickness is often caused by demons, but not always. This verse seems to blur the lines. We have seen men who were deaf and mute; this man was blind and mute. Although it states he was demon-possessed, it doesn't say that Jesus *delivered* him; he was *healed*. Both restore the person to health and free them from affliction, and that is what our ministry should be about.

Once again, the common people marvel at Jesus' power. And, as usual, the religious establishment criticizes. Why is it so hard for them to rejoice at an obvious healing?

²⁴ But when the Pharisees heard this, they said, "It is only by Beelzebul, the prince of demons, that this fellow drives out demons."

When you are not in agreement with what someone is doing, it is convenient to say that it is of the devil. Unfortunately, the Pharisees couldn't see that the same Beelzebub was blinding them and using them to undermine Jesus' ministry. They eventually claimed a short-lived victory as Jesus was crucified, but found themselves fighting God himself!

A house divided

²⁵ Jesus knew their thoughts and said to them, "Every kingdom divided against itself will be ruined, and every city or household divided against itself will not stand. ²⁶ If Satan drives out Satan, he is divided against himself. How then can his kingdom stand? ²⁷ And if I drive out demons by Beelzebul, by whom do your people drive them out? So then, they will be your judges. ²⁸ But if it is by the Spirit of God that I drive out demons, then the kingdom of God has come upon you.

They were probably talking among themselves, and should have been further convicted by Jesus reading their thoughts. He has a concise but convincing rebuttal:

- As the Son of God, Jesus obviously has authority over demons, but in his earthly ministry he relied on the Holy Spirit to drive them out. His life is a demonstration of the same power we have through the Holy Spirit to deliver those in bondage.

- It is implied that Jews also practiced deliverance, although the people seemed unaccustomed to seeing it.

- The kingdom of God is the manifestation of God's reign, and the displacement of the kingdom of darkness. Deliverance is dramatic evidence of God's kingdom being present. If we don't see people set free from demonic oppression, we may question how real the kingdom is in that place.

- Jesus points to a fundamental principle: internal strife leads to a fall. That is why unity is so strongly emphasized in the Bible. How many churches have fallen because of internal divisions! How many families have been devastated!

Plundering the strong man's house

[29] "Or again, how can anyone enter a strong man's house and carry off his possessions unless he first ties up the strong man? Then he can plunder his house.

The strong man is Satan. Don't underestimate him! He is a formidable foe! God wants not only to enter his house, but to plunder it and carry off his possessions, which might be those bound up by demons or blinded to the truth, or those areas of society he dominates. Many well-intentioned believers have attempted church plants, evangelistic campaigns, and other good works, without first binding the strong man. They end up discouraged and even questioning their call or God's power as a result.

Jesus would not have mentioned binding the strong man unless it was possible to do so. But not in your own strength! You will get hurt! You are no match for him, but at the Name of Jesus he has to submit. So how do we go about this?

- First, identify his houses. Prayerfully discern those people or areas where he has built strongholds.

- In united prayer and fasting do warfare to bind him. True unity in the Spirit is necessary to be effective in that prayer. If there is any division in the Lord's army, it will fail. Depending on how big the house is, and how much he has invested in protecting it, he can put up quite a struggle. Many people give up because it is too rough.

- Spiritual discernment is necessary to know when he has been bound, and it is safe to enter the house. It is great to see God respond to our prayers and bind Satan, but many Christians don't realize there is much more to do. That is just the start! Don't leave his house intact! It is like Israel moving into the Promised Land: We need the faith and boldness not only to enter in, but also to retake territory for the Lord.

What is your situation? Are you bound up in a strong man's house? Does he have houses all around you? If you are involved in battle right now, be encouraged! If you need time to regroup, take it. Then get back to the battle! Take some time to prayerfully strategize – preferably with some like-minded brothers or sisters – on plundering his house and taking back the Lord's possessions. Maybe you have a child bound up in the strong man's house. In that case united prayer with your spouse is powerful – and important.

I pray that God would enable you to clearly see what is happening around you in the spiritual realm.

Blasphemy against the Spirit

[30] *"Whoever is not with me is against me, and whoever does not gather with me scatters.* [31] *And so I tell you, every kind of sin and slander can be forgiven, but blasphemy against the Spirit will not be forgiven.* [32] *Anyone who speaks a word against the Son of Man will be forgiven, but anyone who speaks against the Holy Spirit will not be forgiven, either in this age or in the age to come.*

These verses have caused much consternation among believers: Have I been guilty of the unpardonable sin, blasphemy of the Spirit? Jesus is speaking specifically in the context of the Pharisees attributing a work of the Holy Spirit to the devil. I have observed people coming perilously close to that, discounting the Spirit's work among other believers. If you are concerned about committing this sin, chances are you haven't. Blasphemers are self-righteous; so blind that they can't see that healing is God's work, and hardened to the conviction of sin by the Spirit. Paul, for example, may have felt believers were of the devil, but when confronted with the light, he repented. The unforgivable sin may be apostasy; permanently closing your heart to the works of the Spirit, which includes drawing you to Christ and the conviction of sin that leads to repentance. And, in Luke's account (12:8-12), it includes denouncing Jesus under pressure.

Though these verses are sobering, the good news is that there is forgiveness for every other sin and slander! Keep short accounts with God. Make sure any sin is confessed, and then joyfully thank him for his forgiveness, remembering what it cost him.

Verse 30 seems to contradict what Jesus said in Mark 9:40 ("*whoever is not against us is for us*"), but it depends on who Jesus is speaking about. In Mark, people were doing miracles in Jesus' name. Unlike the Pharisees, they were acting through faith in Jesus. And the disciples were jealous!

Jesus is making clear that neutrality is impossible. You are either with him or against him. That is sobering. It places a whole lot of "nice" people squarely against Jesus. You are either gathering with him, or you are scattering. God draws people together and brings peace. Satan brings division and strife.

How is the fruit?

[33] "*Make a tree good and its fruit will be good, or make a tree bad and its fruit will be bad, for a tree is recognized by its fruit.* [34] *You brood of vipers, how can you who are evil say anything good? For the mouth speaks what the heart is full of.* [35] *A good man brings good things out of the good stored up in him, and an evil man brings evil things out of the evil stored up in him.* [36] *But I tell you that everyone will have to give account on the day of judgment for every empty word they have spoken.* [37] *For by your words you will be acquitted, and by your words you will be condemned.*"

Evaluation of a deliverance ministry must go deeper than what is seen in church or on TV. What is their life like? What about their fruit? How is the fruit in their family? How are their relationships with colleagues? What are their conversations like?

What fills your heart? How is that manifest in your speech? What kind of tree are you? What has your fruit been like?

Your mouth can get you in a lot of trouble! Be careful of "empty" words! Think before you speak! You will have to give account for your words!

When a demon returns

Luke 11:14-26 may recount this same incident, although there are several differences. Matthew places these words later in the same chapter (12:43-45); Luke has them in the context of Jesus' teaching on deliverance:

[24] *"When an impure spirit comes out of a person, it goes through arid places seeking rest and does not find it. Then it says, 'I will return to the house I left.'* [25] *When it arrives, it finds the house swept clean and put in order.* [26] *Then it goes and takes seven other spirits more wicked than itself, and they go in and live there. And the final condition of that person is worse than the first."*

The details are clear:

- An unclean spirit is cast out. The person ministering deliverance used the authority Christ gave him, and successfully freed the person.

- Demons hate to leave. It was apparently comfortable in that person, but when he has to leave, he initially seeks rest in "arid places."

- Its inclination is to return to its previous dwelling.

- Perhaps some follow-up was given. The person has apparently been diligent and cleaned house and put it in order.

- There is nothing preventing the spirit from returning to that house; in effect the welcome mat is out.

- The tendency is for the evil spirit to join other, even more sinister, spirits, and go back "home."

- Jesus says they "live there."

- In this case the person ends up worse than before. They have the discouragement of thinking God had delivered them, only to find themselves much worse. You can imagine them getting turned off to Jesus and other believers. They will now be resistant to deliverance, and the satanic oppression is far worse.

Deliverance is not to be taken lightly! Be sure you know what you are doing! You can do untold damage to other people and the kingdom of God.

- There is more to salvation than having someone say the sinner's prayer, and there is more to deliverance than casting out evil spirits. Any Spirit-filled believer can do both, but solid teaching is necessary regarding all facets of the ministry.

- Deliverance should be done in the context of a local body of Christ, where the person is submitted to the leadership and receiving follow-up.

- Part of the deliverance should be prayer for infilling of the Holy Spirit, and teaching on the Spirit-filled life. If they have not been baptized as a believer they should be.

- Someone needs to be in close contact with the person, watching for any indication of the demon returning, and helping them grow in grace.

- When someone who has been doing well suddenly has significant struggles, be alert to the possibility that a spirit has returned, along with others even more destructive. Be ready to confront them and provide additional deliverance.

5   God is with you!

There is one other mention of Jesus' deliverance ministry, in Peter's address to Cornelius in Acts 10:37-38:

You know what has happened throughout the province of Judea, beginning in Galilee after the baptism that John preached— how God anointed Jesus of Nazareth with the Holy Spirit and power, and how he went around doing good and healing all who were under the power of the devil, because God was with him.

Here again deliverance seems to be equated with healing. Peter summarizes Jesus' ministry as healing those under the devil's power, and doing good. He could do that because God was with him, and anointed him with the Holy Spirit and power. And do you know something? God is with you as well! You can experience the same anointing and power! Jesus' life is an example of what God can do with a life that is submitted to him. You can do what Jesus did – and perhaps even more (John 14:12). Although the deliverance ministry is not easy, it is not complicated. We have seen that the key is understanding the authority we have in Christ, and simply speaking in that authority to command the evil spirit to leave. It is our weakness in prayer, fasting, and faith that makes it difficult.

Countless people are suffering under demonic oppression. Christians are busy building empires and having feel-good services, while largely avoiding deliverance. It's too messy, too controversial, and way too demanding. You actually have to be in prayer! And maybe even fast! Meanwhile, families are destroyed, people die, and the church is seen as a joke. Too often healing and deliverance ministries are scorned by the world – and the church. Is it time for you to take them seriously? Do you need deliverance? Does someone that you love?

www.ingramcontent.com/pod-product-compliance
Lightning Source LLC
Chambersburg PA
CBHW060627030426
42337CB00018B/3237